ALIENS
at
Paradise High

Annie Dalton

Illustrated by David Kearney

OXFO
UNIVERSITY

1

Jonah days

It was another grey day in dead-end Greybridge and everything was going wrong. First the batteries in my clock radio had run down. Okay, normally this wouldn't be a big deal. But unfortunately Mum and Dad's alarm didn't go off either. Mum did offer to run me up to school in the car. But, surprise surprise, our car wouldn't start.

I had to run all the way in the pouring rain. I should have got a medal just for turning up. But our head, Mr Griffin's a total meanie so I got a detention instead.

I was still really puffed out from running, when Mr Jackson, our form teacher, said that the school secretary wanted to see me.

Great, I thought. More trouble.

Mum has a special name for those days which start badly and get steadily worse. She calls them 'Jonah days'. There's only one cure. Go back to bed and pull the covers over your head.

Well, since I broke friends with Karen, I'd had a Jonah *term*. Don't get me wrong. I wouldn't be mates with that girl again, not if she came back to our school and begged me. But there's an echoey space inside me where our friendship used to be.

It's embarrassing to tell you this, but I've never been a brave person. On my first day at Greybridge High, my legs totally turned to stewed rhubarb. So when Karen came up to me and asked if I'd let her have a read of my magazine, I almost fainted with gratitude.

It turned out we were crazy about the same soap. After that, the two of us floated around in a world of our own, pretending we were characters in *Paradise High*. My character wrote really deep songs.

That's when I got the crazy idea I could do it in real life. I say crazy, because in the whole of history, no Greybridge kid ever grew up to do anything interesting. It's a law of the universe, like gravity.

Yet the more I day-dreamed about my golden, sunshiny future, the more real it seemed. Everything else was a blur.

Then one day I started to write a story and all my crazy shimmery-gold *Paradise High* feelings poured out. I discovered a totally different Lizzy Lemon. A girl with sparkle and style. A girl who stood up for herself no matter how tough things got. This Lizzy was so alive and real, that for one whole day Greybridge actually turned into Paradise Bay!

But when it was over, Karen and I had a big fight.

I'd never really got to know the other kids at school. So nowadays I go around by myself. No one even sits next to me in class. 'Face facts,' I told myself. 'You're Lizzy No-Mates. Just get used to it.'

I started trudging down the corridor to Miss Simpson's office. Sad Mikey and nerdy Eric were hanging round the computer room. I think they must sleep there.

As I went past the gym, some girls came out and started sniggering. Suddenly I realized who they were laughing at. It was me.

Luckily I was near the girls' toilets, so I dived in and had a bit of a cry. Once I started, it was like defrosting the freezer. Everything flooded out. The day our dog died. The time Mum shrank my new sweater by mistake.

Some girls look cute when they cry. I puff up like a frog. I had to splash cold water on my face for ages. 'Great,' I told my reflection. 'Now you look like a *damp* frog.'

When I finally reached Miss Simpson's office, Mr Griffin's door was open. I could hear some worry-wart mum wittering on. 'You *will* let him use his laptop?' she was saying.

Miss Simpson breezed out. 'Your mum dropped off your lunch,' she said. 'You left it behind.' She gave me a sympathetic look. 'Are you okay, Lizzy?'

I felt my lip wobble. 'Me? I'm fine, Miss,' I gasped. 'It's this allergy.'

I just made it back to the toilets, before I dissolved into a total jelly of self pity. 'You

don't understand,' I snivelled to my
reflection. 'Those dreams were just
dreams. Maybe some
kids grow up to be
famous – or – or
save the world.
But not me.
Not me –'

Then I looked up and saw Mia Turlow in
the doorway. She must have heard me talking
to myself. I nearly died of embarrassment.

'Mr Jackson sent me to find you,' she said.
She didn't look at me, just swished her hair.
Mia is one of the super-cool kids, along with
her big buddy Atlanta.

I kept my head down as I returned to my
seat, so no one could see my froggy face.
Then I heard Mr Jackson say, 'Sit next to

Lizzy for the time being.'

A chair scraped, followed by a tired *flump*. I looked up in alarm.

Karen's empty space had gone. A pale boy was sitting there. Everything about him was pale. Even his eyes were a pale dish water green.

He opened up his laptop computer. With one slow careful finger he typed the day's date, followed by his name. You'll never guess what it was. Muldoon. Jonah Muldoon.

'Forget Jonah days,' I thought in despair. 'It's official. I now have a Jonah *life*.'

Then just when it couldn't get any worse, Jonah spoke to me.

'Psst!' he hissed. 'Do you realize aliens are watching every move we make?'

2

A date with destiny

'Nobody makes girls sit next to boys! Mr
Jackson must really have got it in for me!'

I ranted all through tea. When it was time
for Mum's evening class, she practically ran
out of the house with relief.

'Hey, call that clean?' Dad handed me a
fork with a bean stuck to it.

I swirled the bean down the sink.
'Disappear Jonah Muldoon!' I muttered.

'He was probably trying to do old Jonah a favour,' said Dad. 'Putting him next to the brainiest girl in the class.'

'Yeah, right!' I snorted. I followed him into the living room. 'Actually Jonah's quite smart. He's just so weird. He believes aliens are watching everything we do.'

'He could be right,' grinned Dad. He put on his spooky voice. 'The Truth is out there.' Then he zapped the TV remote and we settled down to watch TV. But there was nothing good on so I went to wash my hair. Hair washing helps me think, I don't know why.

I was still incredibly upset about the Jonah thing. Then I got mad with myself for being upset. 'Are you a girl or a jellyfish?' I asked myself as I lay in bed.

What if I went to school really early? Maybe I could catch Mr Jackson before everyone went into class and tell him how I felt. It wasn't as if he had done it to *spite* me.

'Yeah,' I decided. 'That's what I'll do.' I was

so relieved I drifted into a deep sleep.

Next morning it was actually sunny.
Greybridge doesn't usually do weather. You
know, dramatic stuff like hurricanes and heat-
waves. Most days our town is dull, damp and
grey, like its name.

It doesn't look too bad in sunshine
though. I was in such a great mood, I
practically danced to school. It wasn't just
the sunshine. It was because I'd dropped my
jellyfish routine, and taken control of my
destiny.

'We'll have no more crying in toilets, Lizzy
Lemon,' I told myself. 'Today is the first day
of your real life!'

I knocked at the staff-room door. But Mr
Jackson wasn't there. So I rushed down to our
classroom. He wasn't there either. Guess who
was? Yes, Jonah Early Bird Muldoon.

I felt myself shrivel like a left-over party
balloon. 'What are you doing here?' I said.

Jonah didn't seem to notice how bitter and
twisted I was feeling. 'Oh, hi.' He slung some

magazines on my desk. 'I brought you these.
People should know the facts.' I picked one
up cautiously. It was so soft and creased, he
must have read it about a million times.

'Facts?' I sneered. 'In UFO Monthly?
Everyone knows they make this stuff up.'

He sighed. 'People say those things because
they've been brain-washed.'

'Keep talking like that and everyone will
think you're a loony.'

Jonah smiled a crooked little smile. 'They
think that anyway.'

I felt myself turn red and waved his magazine at him. 'Trust me, normal people do not think about crop circles and hidden codes – and – evil aliens.'

Jonah froze. 'Sssh. Someone's coming,' he hissed.

With an ear-splitting crash, the door flew open. I nearly had a heart attack. It wasn't an alien, of course. It was Mr Jackson, carrying too many books as usual. Mr Jackson's really tall and totally uncoordinated; which makes him a walking disaster area.

'Good to see you two making friends,' he beamed.

I stared at him. Making friends? With *Jonah*? I think Mr Jackson spends too much time watching the Disney Channel.

I slumped in my chair. Last night I had hope. I had a survival plan. Now, everything had fallen apart. Thanks to Jonah I'd completely missed my chance to talk to my teacher.

I caught myself before I spun off into a

Lizzie Lemon Self-Pity Special.

'Has the world ended?' I asked myself sternly. 'I don't *think* so. All you've got to do is catch Mr Jackson at break, instead. It's the first day of your real life, remember!'

Everyone drifted back to their seats and Mr Jackson started taking the register. When he got to Jonah's name, Ash Palmer sniggered, 'Is that the kid from the new estate?' But he did it so Mr Jackson wouldn't hear. Then he leaned over and shoved his face right into Jonah's. 'I'm watching you!' he hissed.

Jonah went white. He started to get out of his seat.

Ash pretended to be scared. 'Oooh! What are you going to do? Hit me with your sad little computer?'

'Leave him alone,' I told him.

'Thanks, I can look after myself,' glowered Jonah.

Just then Mr Jackson clapped his hands. When he gets excited, he looks completely like Bambi. 'I've got fantastic news,' he said.

'Can anyone guess what this is?' He held up a sheet of paper.

'Your resignation, sir,' said Scott.

'You wish,' grinned Mr Jackson. 'Actually it's an entry form for a very special writing competition.'

'Oh, *what*!' groaned Lee.

'Forget it,' said Ash.

But I sat bolt upright.

'The Dream Machine film studios are offering the opportunity of a lifetime,' our teacher went on. 'The two children who come up with the most thrilling, the most unusual, the most action-packed story, will spend a whole day at the studios as their guests.'

'That is so-o cool!' Atlanta whispered to Mia.

I'd totally stopped breathing by now. A fluttery feeling started under my ribs. 'Lizzy, this could be your date with destiny,' I told myself.

'There's just one thing,' Mr Jackson added. 'You've got to work in pairs. So, do some brainstorming first, then write up your ideas with your partner.'

'Ow, can't we do our own, sir?' moaned Bonnie.

'Yeah,' said Lee. 'The other person might have, like – totally different ideas.'

Mr Jackson smiled. 'Those are the ground rules. Film writers quite often work in teams, you know. So I want you to work with the person sitting next to you. Start brainstorming – now!'

I couldn't believe what my teacher had just done to me. A golden opportunity? With Loony Tunes Muldoon as my partner? Yeah, right!

I don't think Jonah was too thrilled either. He cracked his knuckles nervously. 'It's all right. You won't need a pen,' he said. 'I'll type it up as we go.'

My wild fluttery dream had turned into a nightmare.

3

Gobbledygook

'Do you want to start?' Jonah's fingers hovered over the keyboard.

'I can't think if you do that,' I snapped.

He sighed. 'I'll start then.' He did a bit more knuckle-cracking, then saw my face and stopped.

'You'll think this is stupid, okay,' he said awkwardly. 'But I like dead-scary, incredibly confusing stories about aliens and conspiracies, because at the end, all the confusing stuff makes total sense and you feel that bit more hopeful and – and – stronger. Like you could save the planet, like the bloke in the story.'

I stared at him. 'Or like the girl in the story,' I corrected him. I wasn't remotely interested in aliens, but I knew what he meant.

'Or like the girl,' Jonah agreed. 'Obviously.' He was still staring at his trainers. 'I knew you'd think it was rubbish.'

I shook my head. 'Actually, it was all right.'

Jonah flushed. 'It's your turn.'

I suddenly felt tired. 'It won't work,' I said. 'The stories I like are girly and fluffy and you know, LIGHT.'

'So – the stories I like are creepy and lonely and DARK. Ours'll be different. It'll be like, I don't know – *Goosebumps* meets *Hannah Montana*.'

I giggled with surprise. Jonah looked almost human when he smiled. You know, for a weirdo. His joke got me thinking about my favourite soap, *Paradise High*. I found myself telling him about it.

'Remember that book, where they go
through the wardrobe into a snowy forest?
Paradise High isn't just a soap, it is like that,' I
said excitedly. 'It's like a doorway into
another world.'

'But that's how I feel about stories about
UFOs!' said Jonah.
We stared at
each other,
astonished.

After that, our brainstorm went brilliantly.
Ever had that brilliant pudding? Baked
Alaska I think it's called, which is hot and
freezing, creamy and crunchy at the same
time? Our plot was like that. It had absolutely
everything!

The story was set in a sleepy American

town. Aliens love that kind of town, according to Jonah. He had to drag aliens into it, of course. Mind you, for an alien expert, Jonah was surprisingly unhelpful about what they actually *look* like.

'Aliens usually operate behind the scenes,' he explained. 'If too many people saw them, it would start a mega panic.'

I don't know where Jonah got his rigid notion that aliens are always evil. I mean E.T. was cute! Anyway, back to our plot. Our hero was lonely, brave and totally right. But nobody believed him about the aliens. Except for this one girl, who was really popular with everyone. But finally she had to choose between her ditzy friends and trying to save the planet. That part was my idea.

Then I made a fatal mistake. I glanced across at Jonah's laptop to see how he was getting on. The screen was full of gobbledygook.

'Yikes, Jonah! What are you doing?' I yelled. 'Trying to confuse the aliens?'

'You don't have to shout. I'll do a spell check later,' Jonah said. His face was completely blank. Then still without any expression, Jonah hit a button. His screen erupted in a shower of stars.

I was horrified. 'What happened?'

'The system crashed,' he said in a dull voice.

'You did that on purpose!' I lowered my voice to a hiss. 'I *saw* you.'

He shrugged. 'So?'

Honestly, I had to sit on my hands or I'd have thumped him. 'Listen, you!' I snarled. 'I'm not letting you ruin our story with your little tantrum. We're entering this competition if I have to write it myself.'

He shrugged. 'Sure.' He shoved his laptop towards me. Which was a pretty weird thing to do, if you ask me. But nothing that boy did surprised me by now.

It took a few minutes to work out where everything was, then I was ready to begin. All I needed was a title. I hummed and haahed. At last I'd got it.

'ALIENS AT PARADISE HIGH,' I typed.

It was so perfect, I tingled all over. Words came whooshing into my head. Honestly, writing is the closest thing to magic that I know. By the end of the lesson, I was thrilled with myself. 'Do you want me to read it back to you?' I asked Jonah. I'd kind of typed myself out of my bad mood by this time.

But Jonah's face was still stony. 'I'm dyslexic, not stupid.' He read my story with amazing thoroughness, then tossed it back. 'Weren't you listening?' he demanded. 'We won't win. It's a set-up. Everything on this planet is a set-up. Haven't you figured that out yet?'

I'd had about enough of Jonah. 'I bet you think it's a conspiracy if someone's eaten all the Wheatie Puffs, don't you?' I snapped.

'A huge film company like that, asking kids for ideas?' Jonah droned on. 'Lizzy, they're trying to get inside our heads! I mean, it's obvious!'

The only obvious thing to me, was how freaked-out Jonah was acting, since my crack about his spelling.

'Why didn't you say all this when we started?' I objected.

Jonah looked shifty. 'Sometimes I want, you know, a normal life,' he muttered. 'It gets tiring, having to figure out what's going on *behind* everything all the time.'

'Then don't. Look, stop talking about aliens, okay? I'm in a great mood and I refuse to let you ruin it.'

It was true. Writing the story had given me a real boost. For the first time in ages, I could picture a future. A golden, sunshiny future. So what if no Greybridge kid ever became a songwriter? I'd be the first!

Jonah started to shut down the computer. Suddenly he looked totally spooked. 'What's up now?' I sighed.

'Did you notice anything odd when you were using this?' he asked anxiously. 'Weird tingles or anything?'

'Well, yeah,' I said, surprised. 'But writing stuff always makes me feel like that. Don't tell me,' I teased. 'A naughty little alien got inside your computer.'

But he just shook his head. 'I've got this bad feeling.'

Unfortunately Jonah's bad feeling lasted for the rest of the day. By home-time, I was so keen to get away from him, I shot out of school like a speeding bullet.

As I sprinted into the playground, my hair

went whipping across my face. Little piles of dust whizzed about, stinging my ankles. I looked up in surprise. Clouds the size of pillows rushed across the sky.

Jonah rode past, pedalling against the wind like the bad witch in the *Wizard of Oz*. Which is why he didn't see Ash Palmer lurking by the gate. Suddenly there was a clatter and Jonah was on the ground, tangled up with his bike. Ash and his cronies ran off, laughing themselves stupid.

'You morons!' I screamed. I ran to help Jonah. His sleeve had a massive rip in it and there was a gash on his forehead.

He shoved me away. 'Don't *touch* me!' Jonah picked himself up and inspected his bike for damage. The wheel was buckled. 'Great,' he said to himself. 'Gr-eat.' Suddenly he lurched on his feet.

'I'll get someone,' I said.

'Just leave me *alone*!' But he looked totally woozy.

I flagged Miss Simpson down in her shiny new hatchback. 'Miss, Miss! Jonah's hurt!'

We helped Jonah into her car. Miss Simpson and I heaved the bike on to her luggage rack. 'I'll take you home too, Lizzy,' Miss Simpson offered. 'I'm going your way.'

Jonah slumped against his seat, deathly white, until Miss Simpson drove over the speed bumps into the new estate. Then he jerked upright. 'I'll walk from here, thanks.'

We watched Jonah drag his crippled bike across the road. I could tell he was dying for us to go, but Miss Simpson waited until he vanished into a small, terraced house, before driving away.

Greybridge is on a river, and on the drive back we got an amazing view down the valley. By this time, the clouds were moving so fast, the sky looked as if it was boiling.

Then it started to snow. At first just single flakes which melted as soon as they touched the windscreen. Soon they were coming in swarms.

'This weather!' Miss Simpson exclaimed. 'Completely unnatural.'

'Yeah,' I said. 'What happened to global warming?'

By the time we reached my house, Miss Simpson's wipers were doing overtime. 'Thanks, Miss,' I called to her. 'Take care, Miss.'

But as I stood on the slippery pavement, with snowflakes collecting on my eyelashes, I felt a stab of fear. 'She's right,' I thought. 'This weather isn't natural.'

Then a shaft of brilliant light came down from the sky and an unearthly figure strolled out of it.

I stood rooted to the spot, totally numb.

Our door flew open. 'Lizzy, are you mad, standing out here in this storm?' Mum cried. She pulled me into the house.

I turned, like a sleepwalker, to see where the alien had gone.

But there was nothing to see but the falling snow.

4

Pumpkin pie

I didn't tell Mum and Dad about my alien encounter. I couldn't. The sheer unreality of it took my words away.

My parents just thought I was quiet because of getting a chill. They fussed around, running me a hot bath and finding me dry clothes. And by the time things had calmed down, I'd pushed my experience to the back of my mind, in a file marked, *'Think about this later.'*

Mum made this great stew. Usually she's more of a microwave queen. We ate it in front of the telly. But the characters kept disappearing in storms of interference.

Then I remembered it was still the first day of my real life. So I went up to my room and wrote a new song.

It was nothing like my usual style. It was one of those achy breaky country tunes. I was humming it through, when the phone rang.

'Lizzy, it's for you,' Mum called. She covered the mouthpiece. 'A boy in a phone box,' she hissed. 'I told him it was too late, but he says it's urgent.'

I flew downstairs. 'Jonah?' I said cautiously.

'They're here,' he whispered. 'I've seen one, just now.'

Suddenly it was hard to breathe. 'One what?' I asked in my normal voice.

'Sssh,' he hissed. 'An alien, stupid. A beam of light came down, from their mother ship or something, and an alien stepped out of it. I know it sounds unbelievable.'

My heart skipped a beat. *Jonah and I had seen the exact same thing!*

'I believe you, Jonah,' I croaked. 'Actually, I really do.'

'We'll talk tomorrow. Till then, don't trust anybody, okay?' The phone went dead.

When Mum came in to say good-night, I was staring at my ceiling.

'In love?' Mum teased.

'With Jonah? *Please*,' I snorted. But my heart wasn't in it.

Mum switched off my lamp. 'Set your alarm for tomorrow,' she said. 'This storm will probably blow itself out.'

Mum's words were the last thing I heard before I fell asleep.

When I woke up it was still dark. I padded across to my window. It was snowing worse than ever. I couldn't see across the street.

I've always hated the way snow makes even ordinary things like dustbins, look like creepy stand-ins for the real thing. But this snow was something else. Anything could be going on under there, even an alien invasion. And we'd never know until it was too late.

I dived shivering under my quilt and went back to an uneasy sleep. In my dream, Jonah appeared and started lecturing me. 'You shouldn't have written that story,' he yelled. 'Now aliens are taking us over and it's all your fault.'

I woke with a start.

'This is PDS number six zero medium wave. Yes, it's your favourite radio station, comin' atcha 24 hours a day with the tunes YOU love to hear!'

Sun streamed into my room. I sat up groggily.

'It's another crystal clear morning in Paradise Springs, Indiana. And if you woke up with that hungry feeling, why not drop into the Sleepy Dog Diner on your way to work? I hear Rita Mae's got

some maple syrup pancakes that's just dyin' for proper appreciation. Now here's –'

I hit the off-button. Sunny or not, the unusual weather was still interfering with our electrical equipment.

Then I saw the time. 'Oh what! Mr Griffin will go ballistic!'

I leapt up and dashed downstairs.

I'd been hoping our house was buried in a snowdrift. Then I'd have the perfect excuse to stay at home. But to my annoyance the worst of the snow had gone. This morning the town was just prettily frosted, like a huge wedding cake.

Mum and Dad had gone to work without a word. I was really fed up.

'Howdy Lizzy,' called a new neighbour, as I dashed out of our gate. 'Tell your Mom I'll call in to get her recipe for pumpkin pie.'

Presumably this was a joke. I've never had pumpkin pie, but I bet you don't make it in a microwave.

'Mornin',' said Mrs Harris from next door.

'Fixing to get those little songs played on the radio, one day soon?'

'Er,' I said desperately, wishing Mum would stop blabbing my private business.

'Have a nice day now. But get home before dark, do you hear?' Mrs Harris had a strange edge to her voice.

'Oh, Pearl, you didn't ought to be spreading that alien talk,' scolded the pumpkin pie woman.

I stared at them. And for the first time I looked around and saw the extraordinary changes which had taken place during the night.

'This isn't happening,' I told myself.

I took off at a run, my shoes crunching on fine powdery snow, passing unfamiliar wooden houses with front porches and rocking chairs. Finally I reached a road sign.

It said, 'PARADISE SPRINGS, pop: 1200.'

I stared at it blankly. Then I looked down and noticed the huge coat flapping around my ankles. But it wasn't the coat which sent a bolt of terror into my heart. It was the outfit underneath.

'THIS IS NOT HAPPENING!' I screamed.

I set off, running harder than ever. At one point I jumped a trench where someone was installing cable at an old folk's home. There were posters on the trees with the mysterious message: *Because Quantum Cares*.

Who or what is Quantum? I wondered, and why should I care? But still I ran on. Past the bank, the drug store and on past the Sleepy

Dog diner where Rita Mae was serving pancakes to a crumpled-looking man with a sheriff's badge.

And as I ran, I called myself every name under the sun. Jonah *knew* something weird had happened. But would I listen? 'Oh, I always feel tingly when I write!' I mimicked.

Writing isn't CLOSE to magic, Lizzy Lemon, you total idiot. It IS magic. Real, dangerous magic. And that freaky force had mixed up Jonah's weird UFO imaginings with my desperation for something, anything to get me out of my rut.

Now instead of waking up in dull, sensible Greybridge, I was in a small American town in the grip of alien-fever.

My breath streamed out into the sharp pine-smelling air. I'd got a stitch so bad that tears ran down my face. And still I kept on running, but at a slower pace. Because I knew now where I was running to.

I was going to find Jonah, and we were going to get our real town back.

5

Little Miss Popular

As I reached the school, a yellow bus pulled up and dozens of kids spilled out. They were the same kids I saw every day, but about ten times more bouncy. They glowed with health, as if their mothers fed them on buttermilk. They also smiled heaps more than I was used to.

Then my heart stood still. Everyone was smiling at me!

'Lizzy!' yelled a voice. Mia and Atlanta pushed through the crowd. Under their coats they wore tiny sweaters with stars embroidered across the front. Their little pleated skirts only just covered their knickers.

Under my coat, I wore an identical outfit. In this new zappy American version of my high school, Mia and Atlanta were cheer-leaders. And so was I.

Mia slung her arm around my shoulder. 'Lizzy, how come you look so cool? You're the most important member of the team and look at you!'

'Mia Turlow *touched* me,' I thought.

'Did you practise your routine?' asked Atlanta eagerly. 'I did. I practised with my second best pom-poms just about all night.'

'Ooh! Not long now, Lizzy!' sang Mia, shaking her finger teasingly. 'Tonight's the night!' They linked their arms through mine and danced me along as if we were the best of friends.

My head was spinning. Greybridge High is

dead boring, so we just grit our teeth and slog through it. But Paradise High was so happy and fizzy I felt as if I was starring in a Pepsi commercial!

Ash ran past. He grinned bashfully. 'I'll be rooting for ya, Lizzy!'

Mia gave my arm a shake. 'Don't look at him. You know that boy is crazy about you. It's not kind to give him false hope.'

'Absolutely not,' I agreed huskily.

'Hey, Lizzy! Good luck!' called Scott and Lee as we passed.

I scanned the crowd desperately. Where *was* Jonah?

Atlanta and Mia danced me into school. Mia put a coin in a Coke machine and handed me a can smoking with frost.

'Don't drink too fast now. We don't want you burping at an awkward moment,' she giggled.

I knew Mia's friendliness was just a side-effect of my story. So why did it make me feel all pink and fuzzy inside?

As we passed the headmaster's office, I sneaked a look at the trophy cabinet. To judge from the cups stashed in there, the Paradise Pumas had won every game for the past ninety years.

'You should see the cup Quantum donated,' said Atlanta gleefully. 'My daddy says it's the biggest he's ever seen! He says it was a great day when Quantum moved here. He reckons we need to get out of the fifties time-warp and join the rest of the world.'

'I like our little town the way it is,' said

Mia. 'Don't you, Lizzy?'

'This must be what it's like having real friends,' I thought, but aloud I said, 'I don't think I understand what Quantum does.'

'Me neither!' giggled Mia. 'It's WAY too technical!'

Atlanta sighed. 'Everybody knows Quantum is, like – light years ahead in information technology. Computers, mobile phones.'

I couldn't believe it! At Greybridge High, Mia and Atlanta hardly gave me the time of day. Yet here they were, nattering away like chat show hosts!

'What's all that *Quantum cares* stuff mean?' I said, trying to keep up my end of the conversation.

Quantum seemed to be Atlanta's top favourite subject after cheer-leading. Her eyes shone. 'Well, all those old-style businesses were only out to make money. But Quantum believes you can do all that and still be, like – really caring about everything. I mean, they're putting in cable TV for the old folks for free! Isn't that amazing?'

Mia rolled her eyes. 'Lizzy, would you compose a little song to Quantum, so Atlanta can sing it after the game tonight?'

A tiny glow started in my chest. How could this friendly joshing be fake, when it felt so good? 'No problem!' I grinned.

Mia fished a key from a teeny doll's purse round her neck and opened her locker. To my surprise, I had a doll's purse too. When I opened my locker, a bunch of stupid pom-poms fell out. I hastily stuffed them back in. That's when I found Jonah's note. It took a while to decode, but I finally worked out what it said:

Meet me in computer room before class, Jonah.

'Did you see that wild piece in *The Bugle* about aliens?' Bonnie was asking.

'My daddy says *The Bugle* stirs up those rumours on purpose, just to sell papers,' said Atlanta. 'If we don't look out, he says this town will be crawling with alien-watchers.'

Mia grinned. 'Like that creepoid Jonah Muldoon!'

'Remember his first day, when he tried to sit next to you, Lizzy!' Atlanta screamed with laughter. 'And he actually gave you that loony magazine to read!'

I gave a weak smile. Don't get me wrong. I love having mates. I just hate the way someone has to be on the outside, looking in.

Mia's eyes narrowed. 'Lizzy, what are you doing?' she demanded.

I quickly crumpled the note.

'You can't have forgotten we've got a rehearsal first thing! Even you can't be *that* cool!' She presented me with my pom-poms, laughing.

'Could you hang on to them?' I said

suddenly. 'I'll catch you guys later.'

I sprinted off to the computer room where a young man in a beautiful suit was chatting to the IT teacher.

'Hi Lizzy. Good luck for tonight,' said a weedy little voice.

'Thanks,' I said. It was like old times to see Mikey and Eric in there. They looked almost the same as in real life, but with wilder shirts.

'Quantum are installing that new software today,' Eric went on.

'I bet it's just stupid games,' sighed Mikey. 'That stuff is strictly for amateurs.' Honestly, I wanted to hug them.

The man in the suit looked up. He had such a friendly face, I found myself smiling, as if he was someone I really knew.

Then I spotted Jonah,

staring gloomily out at the snow.

I never thought I'd say this, but I was incredibly pleased to see him. At least we were in this together. 'Isn't this all totally insane?' I said. 'But don't worry, we'll soon put it right.' Then I saw his face. 'You look terrible.'

'I couldn't sleep,' he sighed. 'I just lay there trying to figure out what they're up to. And finally I got it. Lizzy, their plan is totally evil.'

'Forget the aliens,' I pleaded. 'We wrote this story, remember? Only I should have known better because – I think something like this happened before –'

But Jonah wasn't listening. 'They'll use some kind of ordinary device,' he droned. 'Something so innocent, no one would suspect it has anything to do with aliens.'

'If your laptop isn't working,' I said desperately, 'a normal pen and paper would be okay.'

Jonah looked annoyed. 'Lizzy, I know

you're everyone's favourite cheer-leader, but could you concentrate for two minutes?'

My mouth fell open. 'You said cheer-leader.'

'Okay, baton twirler. Whatever.' Jonah edged closer so he was practically breathing down my ear. 'Lizzy! It's going on right under all our noses! Without being obvious, take a look around this room and tell me what you see.'

'I see a guy in a suit installing software,' I sighed. 'But Jonah –'

'Exactly,' breathed Jonah. 'Software contaminated with a deadly alien virus, capable of turning anyone who uses it into a total zombie.'

'You're crazy! You don't seriously think the aliens are using Quantum to get at High school kids?'

'I *know* they are. Then they'll take over our town, and –'

'Which town?' I interrupted. 'Tell me which town we're living in.'

'Is this a sanity test? Are you going to ask me the name of the president next?' Jonah backed away from me. 'I thought I could trust you,' he said in a despairing voice. 'Aliens have invaded Paradise Springs and everyone's carrying on as if nothing's wrong. And you think *I'm* nuts?'

'Oh Jonah,' I whispered. 'You totally believe this is real.'

Jonah was muttering frantically to himself. 'Okay, I'll just deal with this by myself. I can do that. I'm not stupid. I'll go and explain everything to Sheriff Tate. I'm going to save this town if it's the last thing I do.' And to my horror, he charged out of the door, still muttering.

'Jonah, wait!' I went chasing after him, but I collided with the man from Quantum.

'Your friend seems rather agitated,' he

said pleasantly.

'Yeah, well, being agitated is like Jonah's full time career,' I said bitterly. 'He's  got this thing about an alien conspiracy. He goes around trying to scare people with it. Sorry, I'd better go after him before he causes any more trouble.'

I brushed past him. The very idea of Jonah running amok, burbling about evil aliens, gave me the total heebie jeebies.

In Greybridge, Jonah Muldoon was just a sad, strange, but basically harmless kid. But in Paradise Springs his weirdness had mutated into something truly alarming – Jonah had actually turned into the misunderstood hero of his worst UFO nightmares – a situation I was fifty per cent responsible for. 'The sooner we write ourselves back home, the better,' I told myself briskly, as I sneaked out of school.

Besides, I didn't know the first thing about being a cheer-leader. There was no reason for me to feel bad about letting Mia and Atlanta down. But as I headed for the sheriff's office, bad was exactly what I felt. Bad, sad and horribly lonely. Maybe this weird parallel existence wasn't real, but it was heaps friendlier than my actual life.

For the first time ever I was little Miss Popular. And I was about to give it all up, for a boy my new friends rated less than a dung-beetle.

6

Lizzy's spooky soundtrack

A monstrous dog lay across the sheriff's step.
It had huge shadows under its eyes, a face
like a Savoy cabbage and it was either a heavy
sleeper or stone dead.

'Step right in,' someone called. 'But I'll
warn you, if my dog suspects you of double
dealin', she'll likely have your leg off.'

But as I approached, the dog just opened one bloodshot eye and thumped her tail, so I went in.

The sheriff looked so like his dog, it was hard not to stare. 'Oh, it's you, Lizzy,' he growled. 'Mind tellin' me what you're doin' off school? Today's your big day ain't it?'

I wished everyone would stop saying that. It made me feel really guilty for not being the pom-pom princess everyone thought I was.

'I'm looking for Jonah,' I said.

'I sent him back to school. Boy has this dingbat obsession with aliens.' The sheriff sighed. 'All this wild alien talk makes everyone jumpy and jumpy folk can't think straight.'

I decided against telling the sheriff I'd seen an alien too. 'What would you do if you saw one?' I asked.

'Set my dog on them, I reckon.' The sheriff gave a rusty chuckle. 'You think I'm kidding. That's because you ain't never seen Dolly with her dander up.'

'Is Dolly the dog they named the diner after?'

'Lord, no. That one died more than thirty years ago. Dolly comes from a long line of Sleepy Dogs. Couldn't maintain law and order without 'em.'

'Shouldn't I have seen Jonah on the way here, if he went back to school?' I asked anxiously.

'Tell you what. Let's step next door and ask Rita Mae if she's seen him,' said the sheriff. 'Nothing generally gets past her. Besides I could use a cup of coffee.'

The diner was packed with workmen yelling things like, 'I prefer my eggs over easy, Rita Mae.'

Rita Mae pushed the coffee pot across the counter. 'Help yourselves,' she told us. 'Or you'll sit waitin' till Doomsday. These cable TV fellers have powerful appetites.'

The young man from Quantum with the nice smile came in and studied the Specials board.

'Lizzy, you're as skinny as a rail,' Rita Mae scolded. 'Have a slice of apple pie before you disappear entirely.'

The Sleepy Dog smelled warm and spicy, as if she was baking pies at this moment. My breakfast had consisted of a can of coke. My stomach rumbled hopefully. 'I'd love some,' I said.

'Lizzy reckons Jonah's gone dashing off on some wild goose chase,' the sheriff yelled, over the sound of sizzling ham.

'Last I saw, he was heading out towards Heavenly Creek,' Rita Mae called. She handed me my slice of pie. 'Want a scoop of ice-cream with that?' she said.

I told myself I'd be no use to Jonah if I fainted from hunger. So while the sheriff and Rita Mae chatted, I sat at the counter, stuffing my face. But the longer I sat there, the worse I felt.

You know those scenes in films where the characters are having a totally wonderful time? Then one by one scrapy violins sneak on to the soundtrack, until you're so on edge, you want to scream, 'RUN BEFORE IT'S TOO LATE!'

It was like that. The sun poured in the windows like maple syrup, only with extra dazzle from bouncing off the snow outside.

Ham sizzled, cutlery clattered. The sheriff and Rita Mae smiled bashfully into each other's eyes.

But underneath, invisible violins were going berserk. No one but me seemed to notice.

The Quantum man got up and walked to the door. 'Sorry, Rita Mae,' he said. 'I'll have to leave those pancakes for another day. I'm running late. Why, Lizzy,' he added, looking delighted to see me. 'You ran off so fast, I

didn't get the chance to wish you well for tonight.' And shrugging an elegant coat over his suit, he walked out.

Rita Mae and I both gazed after him. 'If I had a big brother, I'd want him to be exactly like that,' I thought wistfully.

'Mr Octavius has such beautiful manners,' sighed Rita Mae. 'I tell you, his company is the best thing to happen here since the rail road.'

'Yeah yeah, Mr O's a regular saint,' said the sheriff. 'Just hope you all like him so much when you wake up to find he owns this whole town and everyone in it.'

'Aw, Dwayne,' said Rita Mae. 'What have you got against him?'

'I don't trouble my mind one way or the other,' said the sheriff innocently. 'It's Dolly who can't abide him.'

'Erm, are Quantum's offices near here?' I asked, trying to sound casual.

'They've converted some old luxury hotel out at Heavenly Creek,' said Rita Mae. 'I hear it is out of this *world*.'

'I'd better go now,' I said. 'Thanks for the pie.'

I hung around outside until I judged the sheriff and Rita Mae had forgotten about me. Then I doubled back.

I soon found the signpost to Heavenly Creek. Suppose Jonah was storming into Quantum right this minute, making a complete twit of himself? I felt bad about wasting so much time.

I jogged along through sparkling picture-book snow for twenty minutes or more, but there was no sign of him.

I started imagining what Mia and Atlanta would say when they realized I'd let them down. Of course, if I had turned up, I'd *still* have let them down, with my humiliating lack of cheer-leader skills.

'You are such a fluff-brain, Lizzy,' I scolded myself. 'It's Jonah you should be worrying about.' But next minute, Jonah dropped off my worry list, because suddenly a shaft of

light came down and an unearthly figure
stepped out in front of me.

It was my alien.

7
Aliens!

Lately I'd heard enough alien talk to last my whole life. Bright lights, deadly devices, evil plans to take over humanity; blah blah blah.

But when I got over the shock, the alien didn't look much different to humans. Admittedly its hair was pretty funky, but its face was so sweet and calm, it wouldn't have looked out of place on an angel. I was also fairly sure 'it' was a 'she'.

Suddenly the alien cracked up. 'Your face!' she cackled. 'Any minute now, you'll ask me to take you to my leader!'

I stared at her. At no point had Jonah given the impression that aliens had a sense of humour. She shivered. 'Aren't you freezing in that tiny skirt? Let's go back to my ship and talk in comfort.'

I was horrified. 'Your *ship*? You want me to walk up that –'

'Relax.' She gave a crisp command and a
beam of light came down. Before I knew
what was happening, the alien grabbed my
hand.

Honestly, someone should have captured it
on video. Me, Lizzy Lemon, walking up the
sky hand in hand with an actual alien!

At the end of the light-beam, a door slid open. I ducked through it into a cabin full of computers and flashing lights.

The alien threw herself into a strange chair and patted one beside her. 'Glad to meet you finally,' she grinned. 'We've been interested in you for some time.'

'You made a mistake then,' I said sassily. 'I'm not a bit interesting.'

She didn't seem at all offended. 'Oops, I forgot to introduce myself,' she said. 'I'm Macey Kantaria. The thing is, I've been hoping to run in to you, Lizzy. My people could use your help.'

I jumped to my feet. 'I'm not helping you take over my planet,' I said. 'No way!'

Macey started to giggle, then sobered up. 'Actually, this IS my planet. Just not my time frame.'

I stared at her. 'You're not an alien?'

'Uh-uh.' Macey shook her head.

'What – are you from the future or something?'

'WAY into your future,' she said. 'Which probably makes us seem like a different species. But we're really just you, just further down the line.'

I went a bit woozy at that point, so Macey broke off to get me something to drink. 'Poor Lizzy,' she said. 'It's a lot to take in at once.'

I had a cautious sip from my glass, then felt like a real berk. It was fizzy lemonade!

It turned out Macey was some sort of troubleshooter, working for a secret government department.

'What I mostly do is travel back in time,' she explained. 'Trying to catch small problems, before they get big enough to do serious damage.' She whizzed her chair over to a machine and tapped in a code. 'Let me show you something.'

Suddenly I was looking at a map of Paradise Springs. I could make out the bank and the sheriff's office. It was strangely alive for a map. Restless lights and shadows kept sweeping across it.

'What do those grungy colours mean?' I
asked uneasily.

'I'm afraid it's a bad sign,' sighed Macey. 'It
means that huge quantities of human fear are
pumping through this little town and out
into the planet's atmosphere.'

'Yeah, right!' I grinned. Then I realized she
wasn't kidding.

'That's why I've been sent here,' Macey
explained. 'Fear busting is kind of my
speciality.'

'Fear busting?' I said, still disbelieving. 'But fear is just a feeling.'

'To humans,' she agreed. 'But to some alien life-forms, fear is food.'

'You're kidding!' I said.

'Fear is just energy, right? Energy is fuel. All life forms, and all machines need fuel. These little creepoids run on fear. Some years ago, their stocks ran out. They can't manufacture it themselves. They don't have emotions. So they decided to 'grow' their food on some other planet. This planet, Lizzy.'

I stared at her. 'Like a fear-farm, you mean? Ugh, that's so sick.'

'Usually they get some low-life human to do their dirty work for them,' said Macey. 'They promise him untold wealth, the usual thing, and in return he beams them a steady supply of human fear.'

This was getting too creepy for words. 'But where do I come in?' I said. 'I mean, this is my story, right?'

Macey grinned. 'That's where you're wrong,' she said. 'Lizzy, didn't you wonder how you and Jonah wound up in Paradise Springs?'

'I thought – because I wrote that story.'

She shook her head. 'It's not your writing, Lizzy. It's your imagination. You actually have the power to make dreams come true. Only this time those aliens have somehow managed to turn your dream into a nightmare.'

'I'm dreaming all this,' I thought dizzily. 'I am definitely dreaming.'

'According to my sources, your abilities are way ahead of your time,' Macey continued. 'But having such unusual powers naturally makes you feel pretty lonely and confused. So you try to blank them out.'

I felt as if I'd walked into a scene from Star Trek Voyager. Macey was being dead personal. Yet somewhere inside, what she was saying made a strange kind of sense.

'Something happened before,' I said slowly.

'I thought it was a dream. A wonderful impossible –'

I broke off. Grungy yellow swirls had begun to pour from the fear map. Macey whistled.

'Where's it coming from?' I asked anxiously.

Macey frowned. 'It's the school. Did you notice anything unusual before you left?'

'Just some guy installing new software,' I said carelessly. Then a terrifying thought hit me like a runaway truck.

'Lizzy?' said Macey.

'I am so STUPID,' I gasped out.

Macey stared at me.

'I thought Jonah was just, you know, being Jonah. Only crazier. He's always spouting conspiracy stuff. If you believed it all, you'd go nuts. How was I to know he was actually on the right track.' I clutched my head. 'So that's why I heard violins!'

'Violins?' echoed Macey.

'He seemed so NICE,' I wailed. 'I wanted

him to be my big brother.'

'Lizzy!' yelled Macey. 'I'll strangle you if you don't spit it out!'

I wrung my hands. 'That low-life human, who does all the aliens' dirty work. I know who he is.' I swallowed hard. 'It's Mr Octavius.'

8

Nightmares

Macey made me tell her everything I knew about Quantum. Then she grabbed her bag of fear busting equipment and we beamed down to Paradise High.

The moment I stepped out of the beam I could feel the panic pulsing through the air, like a runaway heartbeat.

Macey's face was grim. 'Let's go and see your headmaster,' she said.

But when I knocked on Mr Griffin's door, there was no reply. I pushed the door open. His office was empty. The phone dangled from its flex.

'Weird,' I whispered.

Macey and I ran down silent corridors, peering in the classrooms. But they were all empty. The lights kept flickering eerily.

'Something's overloaded the power supply,' said Macey.

'Where *is* everyone?' I whispered.

Suddenly the intercom crackled and Mr Griffin's voice boomed out. 'Alien alert. Alien alert. Any staff or children remaining in the school should make their way quickly and calmly to the shelter. I repeat any staff or children '

I stared at Macey. 'This can't be happening.'

'It isn't,' she said crisply. 'Come on, I need to check out the computers.'

The computer room had clearly been evacuated in a hurry. Chairs were strewn all over the place. The machines were still switched on. Eerie patterns flickered across the screens.

'Don't touch them,' Macey ordered. 'Don't even look at them. Alien viruses are tricky things.'

Macey got out her fear busting kit and ran a routine check on the school system.

Which left me with nothing to do except play a depressing game of 'If only.'

If only I hadn't written the story. If only I'd listened to Jonah. Then the whole school wouldn't be panicking about an imaginary alien invasion; while Octavius merrily sold them out to the real ones.

Macey took off her headset, looking harassed. 'It's worse than I thought,' she said. 'It's their software all right. But the actual fear impulses are coming from outside the school.'

Just then I heard a sound. 'There's something outside, in the corridor,' I hissed. I saw Macey's eyes widen, as we listened to the creature pad closer and closer in the kind of slow-motion that only happens in nightmares. I could hear the clicking of its huge horrible claws.

'Macey,' I quavered.

The door burst open and a cabbage-faced
dog shambled in, her toenails clicking like
castanets. 'Dolly. You gave me a heart-attack,'
I told her. Dolly collapsed beside Macey with
a heavy sigh, and fixed her with tired but
adoring eyes.

Sheriff Tate stormed in. 'I got some hoax call about an alien attack!' he barked. 'Will someone tell me what in tarnation is going on?'

Then, for the first time, the sheriff got a good look at Macey. There was an awkward pause. 'You're not from round here, Miss, are you?' he said at last.

'You tell him, Macey,' I said. 'You can

explain the scientific bits better than me.'

The sheriff listened to Macey's story in utter silence. But as she went on, his face got tireder and more crumpled. 'Miss Macey,' he said, when she'd finished. 'That's the most scandal-mongering tale I ever heard. A respected businessman in cahoots with aliens? Do you really expect me to swallow that?'

We stared at him in dismay.

He sighed. 'However, I do. And not because of your highly futuristic words, though they did sound mighty fine.'

Macey looked bewildered. 'Why then?'

'Dolly hasn't taken her eyes off you,' explained the sheriff. 'But the first time Mr O came to say howdy, she kicked up such a ruckus, I knew then that he was a real snake in the grass. Plus I could never understand how someone so darn NICE got to be such a hotshot business man in the first place. You could say I was playin' a bit of a waitin' game.'

He gave a dark chuckle. 'But now I'm going straight over to Quantum to take a real good look around.' He strode towards the door. 'By the way Lizzy,' he said. 'Ever catch up with young Muldoon?'

Suddenly I broke out in goosebumps. 'Jonah!' I stammered. 'H-he's gone to Quantum all by himself.'

The sheriff stopped dead.

Macey gasped. 'Why didn't you say!' She ran her hands through her hair, making it look more other-worldly than ever. Then she appeared to make up her mind about something. 'Lizzy, you know when we talked about your powers?'

I nodded unhappily.

'That wasn't the whole truth. Jonah has the same gift. With one crucial difference. You create what you long for, Lizzy. It very much looks as if Jonah is conjuring up what he most fears.' Macey frowned. 'Lizzy, can you remember *saying* anything about Jonah to Octavius?'

'Yes,' I whispered. 'I said he made a career out of being scared.' My lip quivered. 'I betrayed him.'

But Macey had stopped listening. 'Sheriff,' she said suddenly. 'Is there anyone around here who might have an extra-large mainframe computer?'

The sheriff scratched his head. 'Well, I ain't no Einstein,' he said shyly. 'But if it was me, I'd check out the Quantum building.'

'Then could we tag along?' Macey asked. 'Until we track down the source of the problem, we don't have a hope of getting the school back to normal.'

We piled into the sheriff's ancient Chevy and roared off to Heavenly Creek. The sheriff immediately got on the radio, to call for back-up. Macey just stared at the snowy highway rushing by, without a word.

Suddenly I couldn't bear the look on her face. 'It'll be all right, won't it?' I pleaded. 'Once you find that computer everything will be okay?'

'Lizzy, the computer isn't the source,'
Macey's voice was frighteningly quiet.
'Computers can't generate fear. Only people
do that.'

My heart gave a lurch. 'You mean all this is
coming from *Jonah*? Octavius is using Jonah's
panic to – infect the school?'

I couldn't believe I'd trusted such an evil
man, purely on the basis of lovely clothes
and a beautiful smile. Now thanks to me,
Jonah was hooked up to some sinister
Quantum computer. Something I wouldn't

deliberately do to my worst enemy.

And Jonah was my friend, I realized suddenly. My totally weird, brave, scared friend.

The Chevy rattled to a halt. 'Want to stay here, Lizzy?' grunted the sheriff.

But I shook my head. 'You're kidding,' I said. 'I *have* to go.'

We crunched through the snow to the main entrance. From the outside, Quantum looked incredibly expensive and glossy.

But before we reached the door, a shadow fell across the snow. 'Quite a deputation,' said a pleasant voice. 'What can I do for you good people?'

When I saw Octavius smiling his big brother smile, something snapped inside me. 'You monster!' I yelled. 'Take us to Jonah right now!'

'Lizzy seems over-excited,' Octavius said to the sheriff. 'You should take her home.' He blipped a remote. With an electronic hum, the Quantum building sealed itself efficiently against intruders.

'In fact,' Octavius said, in the same pleasant, amused voice. 'I think you should all go home. After all, what *would* you charge me with?' he asked the sheriff.

The sheriff's brow crumpled. 'Dang, you're right,' he said. 'There ain't nothing in the law books says a man can't sell his fellow humans to evil aliens. That's what you call a stinker, Dolly, ain't it?' he said, giving her a loving pat. Dolly looked up and a quiver of excitement went through her. The sheriff gave her the tiniest nod.

'You're a fool, Dwayne Tate,' said Octavius. 'That kid's terror is like a whirlpool, sucking in the fears of everyone at Paradise High.' He laughed. 'And it's all thanks to Lizzy here. She gave me the idea of using Jonah,' he added.

I thought I'd die of shame. But then, just when everything seemed completely hopeless, I heard a rumble, like far-off thunder.

I stared down at the sheriff's dog. But Dozy Dolly had vanished. In her place was the Hound from Hell.

Bristling hairs stuck up along her spine, making Dolly seem twice her normal size. Her ears lay flat against her skull, giving her a wolf-like appearance.

Octavius stepped backwards nervously.

Dolly gave another, far more ferocious growl. Her top lip curled back to show dripping fangs. Suddenly she hurled herself at Octavius. I heard a shocked 'ouf' sound as all the air left his lungs.

'Get her off me, Tate!' Octavius shrieked.

The sheriff shook his head. 'Someone's got to keep an eye on you until the feds get here. They'll be interested to hear about the kidnapping of young Jonah.'

Muffled protests came from beneath Dolly's enormous backside. 'You'll never get inside the building,' Octavius raged. 'Quantum is a space age fortress. It has every possible warning system.'

Macey's expression was unreadable. 'Space age to you, maybe,' she said sweetly. 'But quaintly old-fashioned to me.'

She took a teeny egg-timer out of her pocket and pointed it at the door. The door obediently slid open.

'Ready, Lizzy?' said Macey. 'Then let's go and find Jonah.'

9

Special powers

We found him strapped to a chair,
staring straight ahead.

'Jonah!' I called. 'It's okay.
We're here.'

But he didn't turn to
look at me. Directly in
front of him, was a huge
and terrifyingly
complex computer.
But Jonah wasn't
looking at that either. He
wasn't looking at
anything real. His face was
totally covered by a virtual
reality helmet.

I rushed to him, but an
invisible wall sent me
staggering back.

'It's some kind of force-field,' said Macey.

'The bad news is, the computer's inside it too.'

'It's okay, Jonah,' I babbled.

Macey shook her head. 'He can't hear you.'

'Because of that helmet?'

'Because he's scared to death,' she said.

Macey soon discovered a major problem. She couldn't get through the force-field to disconnect Jonah from the alien computer. And if she couldn't touch the computer, there was no way to bring down the force-field. Macey tried everything she knew. But nothing worked.

The longer I looked at Jonah's pale face under that hideous helmet, the worse I felt. 'He's so lonely,' I thought. 'He's absolutely the loneliest person I know.'

Suddenly I went over and sat on the floor, as close to Jonah as I could get. And without warning, words started to spill out of me.

'I should have listened,' I said. 'You were right about Quantum. I thought you were nuts to be so suspicious. I was wrong.'

I swallowed. 'Jonah, I know you think you're stupid and – and – some kind of freak. But the fact is, you and me, we've got these incredible special powers. I'm not kidding. There's only one thing stopping you from fear-busting your way out of this. And it's you. And I'm going to let you think about that for a while, okay?'

And then I did something really peculiar. I closed my eyes and I sang to Jonah.

It was my new song; the achy breaky one. And while I sang, I reminded myself that I had the power to make dreams come true.

Dreams, not nightmares.

Suddenly I heard a strangled noise. I opened my eyes nervously.

It was coming from inside Jonah's helmet.

Horribly out of tune, but with loads of feeling, Jonah was singing my song back to me! By the final verse, he was bellowing like a football fan.

And with a massive electronic sigh, the force-field expired.

Macey rushed over. 'What did you do?' she demanded.

'I told Jonah *he* had to fear-bust himself out of it,' I said. 'So he did.'

The weird thing was that after we'd unhooked him from the alien computer, Jonah looked totally brilliant.

I mean he was shaky obviously. But for the first time since I'd known him, he looked straight at me. And I saw something in his eyes that hadn't been there before. Special powers, I thought. Jonah's special powers.

He looked incredibly shy. 'I owe you, Lizzy,' he said huskily.

'No, you don't,' I told him. 'I should have listened to you.'

The sheriff cleared his throat. 'Include me in that apology.'

But we still had the tiny problem of what to do about the evil aliens. Everyone racked their brains. 'It's not enough to disconnect them from their food supply,' said Macey. 'We've got to stop them even *wanting* to contact this planet ever again.'

'That's not hard,' said Jonah. 'If fear is what gives them a buzz, why not plug them into the other end of the spectrum? You know, a really feel-good feeling!'

'You mean, hit them with happiness?' I started to grin. 'That's such a cool idea!'

'Any ideas how we'd do that?' asked Macey

I couldn't stop giggling. 'I have. But we're going to need a radio.'

'I've got a radio in the car,' said the sheriff.

He fetched it and Maccy got busy connecting it up to the giant computer. 'You do the honours, Jonah,' she said at last.

'*Yess*,' said Jonah. And he hit the on switch.

'*– coming atcha 24 hours a day with the tunes you love to hear,*' blared a breezy voice.

'Apologies for the bad reception, due to some unusual weather conditions. But now we have another crystal clear afternoon in Paradise Springs, and I'll soon be taking you live to the Pumas' game. But first here's a golden oldie for ya!'

The air filled with guitars, and a honey-sweet voice began to sing about love and home and happiness.

We tiptoed away, leaving the radio at full blast.

I imagined the relentlessly cheerful sound, travelling out into deep space, past empty moons and blazing suns, into strange unnamed galaxies. 'Poor aliens,' I said. 'Imagine ordering fear-burgers and getting Paradise Radio.'

'Coming atcha twenty-four hours a day!' hooted Jonah. 'With the tunes you LURVE to hear.'

Macey casually slung an arm around each of us. 'Okay, fellow fear busters! Want a lift back to good old Greybridge?'

I shook my head. 'Not yet,' I said spookily. 'None of us can leave Paradise Springs just yet.'

'Why?' Jonah looked nervous.

I cracked up laughing. 'Because we're going to the Pumas' game, silly!'

It wasn't really cheating for me and Jonah to use our powers to give ourselves a happy ending. And if it was, well, it was worth it!

After everyone came out of the bunker and the sheriff told them what Octavius had been up to, Mia and Atlanta totally forgave me.

As for Ash Palmer and his cronies; well, they were forced to see Jonah in a whole new light.

And that brings me to my big moment, when I finally got to do all the shamelessly fluffy things the Paradise Springs Lizzy was famous for.

It was brilliant marching into the stadium, hearing the roar of the crowd and looking up to see Jonah and Macey, waving like crazy. How did I do? Well if you really want to know, I was a total star!

I smiled and sparkled. I flounced and twirled. And as I belted out our sassy Pumas' chant, I felt as if I'd been a pom-pom princess all my life.

'Paradise Pumas are the BEST.
We'll beat you first,
and then we'll beat the REST!'

Then it came. The part of the routine where Atlanta and Mia carefully stood upright on the shoulders of the other three. There was a drum roll. And suddenly it was happening. My team-mates were pulling me up through the air. Up and up and up.

Until there I was, straight-backed, smiling and utterly still, at the top of a human pyramid!

I knew the moment wouldn't last. I knew that after the game was over, I'd find myself back in Greybridge with my feet on the ground, getting on with my real life. But that was cool. Because now that I was a qualified fear buster with special powers, I could do anything I put my mind to.

And if some people thought Jonah and I were sad or weird, that was their hard luck.

Because the truth is, we're simply that little bit ahead of our time.

About the Author

I sympathize with Jonah, the lonely UFO-freak in *Aliens at Paradise High*. When I was growing up, my imagination was like a panicky pony, constantly running away with me. Luckily, like Lizzy, I discovered I could channel my scary daydreams into writing stories and life became much calmer!

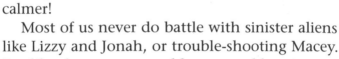

Most of us never do battle with sinister aliens like Lizzy and Jonah, or trouble-shooting Macey. But like them we are real heroes and heroines, as we learn to choose the futures we truly want, and not the ones we fear.